For the Record

and other Poems of Hong Kong

This collection of sixty poems, FOR THE RECORD, was written during almost thirty years' residence in Hong Kong. Most are on explicitly Hong Kong topics, and reflect the writer's personal experience and knowledge of Hong Kong. Those who have emigrated or who have spent a period of time overseas will empathise with the expatriate experience described. Other poems narrate and reflect on personal events and concerns which will resonate with many. The first edition, published in 2003, was supported by Hong Kong Arts Development Council.

GILLIAN BICKLEY is the author of several books on Hong Kong topics, including the well-received short history of early Hong Kong Government education, told through the life of its founder, *The Golden Needle: The Biography of Frederick Stewart (1836-1889)*, first published by the David C. Lam Institute for East-West Studies, Hong Kong Baptist University, in 1997, *Hong Kong Invaded! A '97 Nightmare*, a new illustrated edition of the previously long-forgotten 1897 account of the fictional invasion of Hong Kong in the same year, published by the University of Hong Kong Press in 2001, and *The Development of Education in Hong Kong 1841-1897 as Revealed by the Early Education Reports of the Hong Kong Government 1848-1896*, published by Proverse Hong Kong in 2002, supported by the Council of the Lord Wilson Heritage Trust, and distributed by the Chinese University of Hong Kong Press. She has lived in Hong Kong since 1970, with a couple of years' break, when she was on the faculty of the University of Auckland, New Zealand. At the time the first edition of *For the Record* was published she was Associate Professor in the Department of English Language and Literature at the Hong Kong Baptist University, where she taught from 1982 to 2004. She has previously also taught at the University of Lagos, Nigeria and the University of Hong Kong. With Verner Bickley, Gillian Bickley is one of four voices in the full audio recording of a set of three poetry anthologies, edited by Verner Bickley, *Poems to Enjoy*, published by Hong Kong Educational Publishing Company, and one of two voices in the full audio recording of the expanded five book set of *Poems to Enjoy*, published by Proverse Hong Kong, 2012-2015 For many years, she was an adjudicator at the Hong Kong Schools' Speech Festival and was one of the panel of Adjudicators at the 1999/2000 Hong Kong Poetry Competition, organized by the Royal Commonwealth Society, of which Verner Bickley was then the Chairman and David Tang the President.

For the Record

and Other Poems of Hong Kong

Gillian Bickley

Proverse Hong Kong

For the Record, and other Poems of Hong Kong
by Gillian Bickley.

3rd & revised pbk edition published in Hong Kong by Proverse Hong Kong,
1 March 2021
Copyright © Gillian Bickley 2021.
ISBN-13: 978-988-8492-23-7

First published in pbk in Hong Kong by Proverse Hong Kong, 2003,
accompanied by two audio CDs containing the author's professionally-
recorded reading of all sixty poems in the collection
and supported by Hong Kong Arts Development Council.
Copyright © Gillian Bickley 2003
ISBN-10: 962-85570-2-5; ISBN-13: 978-962-85570-2-8
2nd pbk edition (no CDs) published in Hong Kong by Proverse Hong Kong,
22 February 2016. ISBN: 978-988-8228-30-0
Various Ebook editions

Distribution (Hong Kong and worldwide):
The Chinese University Press, The Chinese University of Hong Kong,
Shatin, New Territories, Hong Kong SAR.
E-mail: cup@cuhk.edu.hk; Web: www.cup.cuhk.edu.hk
Distribution (United Kingdom): Stephen Inman, Worcester, England.
Email: ukagent@proversepublishing.com

Enquiries to: Proverse Hong Kong,
P.O. Box 259, Tung Chung Post Office, Tung Chung,
Lantau Island, NT, Hong Kong SAR, China.
E-mail: proverse@netvigator.com; Web: www.proversepublishing.com

British Library Cataloguing in Publication Data.
A catalogue record for the 1st edition of this book is available
from the British Library.

Preface

Although this book of poetry is addressed to all readers, there is one particular group among these, whom I represent, and this is why I have pleasure in offering this Preface.

Founded in 1940, the Hong Kong Schools Music and Speech Association has successfully encouraged large numbers of Hong Kong teachers and students to take an interest in Chinese and Western speech, drama, poetry and prose. Its annual Speech Festival, which takes place in 2003 for the fifty-fifth time, has introduced hundreds of thousands of Hong Kong young people to a wide variety of poetry and prose, written in English and Chinese, in a range of styles, on many topics, and evoking different moods, thoughts and emotions. For the past few years, the English Speech Selection Sub-Committee has issued an invitation to Hong Kong writers, soliciting, for the Festival, "Poems from Hong Kong for Hong Kong". This collection of poems takes up the challenge.

Literature is one of the most effective ways of conveying and receiving experience and vision. There is enormous value for the Hong Kong students in our member schools in preparing, for the annual Speech Festival, pieces written from, and for, other places, other minds, and other times, but there is also solid value for them in seeing what may be written about their own place and time, and realizing that literature is what we *all* may produce.

The value to Hong Kong teachers and students of this particular collection is enhanced further by the accompanying recording of the full text of all the poems, read by the writer herself. Well read, carefully and clearly, giving expression to the mood of the words, this audio text will help students learn correct pronunciation and also give them some indications of how the phrasing and rhythm of a reading, in particular, need to be carefully studied to reflect and communicate the written meaning on the page.

I am grateful that the publisher offered a copy of the first edition of this book to secondary school members of the HKSMSA, through the Association, and I am confident that it is a useful means of encouraging teachers and students to consider

Hong Kong — their own city and their own countryside, themselves, their own families and fellow citizens, flora and fauna — as valuable subjects for literature. Additionally, I hope that teachers and students will be confirmed in their understanding that acquiring excellent skill in the English Language is a community service as much as it is a personal advantage. We need to communicate with the outside world, and to give them our own many visions of Hong Kong, to win friends and understanding within the international community. How better to do this, for the next many years, than through excellent English?

But this collection also stands alone as a contribution, beyond the schoolroom and the speech festival, to what is written about Hong Kong.

Gillian Bickley presents the Hong Kong cityscape from a thoughtfully "green" perspective, looking through the concrete to show the natural world that our modern buildings replace or embrace. As Dave McKirdy, convenor of the Hong Kong poetry group, "OUTLOUD", has written for *The Asian Review of Books*, Gillian Bickley's work, "offers a counterpoint of the survival and continuity of nature against which our busy everyday lives are measured. Bickley's Hong Kong is both a universal and a personal one . . . she captures a Hong Kong of the mind; the one city that we all share as a physical space against the myriad cities that we experience and perceive distinctly as our own."

Rosanna Wong, PhD, DBE, JP
President
Hong Kong Schools Music and Speech Association

Table Of Contents

Acknowledgements

Verner Bickley, as always, has been generously supportive both in work and in life.

Warm thanks go also to Francine Baker, Annie Chan, Pam Clarke, Simon Chau, Peter Gordon, Nicole Ho, Agnes Lam, S. H. Lee, Gloria C. H. Ng, Tracy Liang, Dave McKirdy, Andrew Parkin, Silvie Taylor, Jonathan Tse, Tse Kwok Hay, Wai Sing-fat and Rosanna Wong Yick-ming.

Prior Publication Acknowledgements

'Swallows, *Dimsum* (the Journal of good reading), Ed. Nury Vittachi, Hong Kong, Chameleon Press Ltd., Vol. 1, No. 3, 2000, pp. 71-72.

'Death Bed Wisdom', English Department Student Journal, Hong Kong Baptist University, 2002.

'Ching Ming Festival, April the Fifth, 1991', English Department Student Journal, Hong Kong Baptist College.

Welcome

Writing poetry is a good way to
communicate in this busy world. In the
interstices of appointments, duties, transport connections
and pleasures,

memories recur, are
dwelt on, interpreted, revised; until,
one day, you make it known that you
would like to hear something from me.

And there they are, waiting for me,
ready to be written down, quite quickly, and

handed over to you
efficiently,

— the sweets and pills of my life, which you can
swallow, absorb, or pass—on—
without giving them much of
your time

either.

March 2000

For The Record

On a showing of slides of images of old Hong Kong kept in the Hong Kong Public Records Office, then newly established.

We sit in a darkened room,
gazing at the bright screen, where
images of old Hong Kong appear.

An eerie silence drains the scenes:
Few people; little life that moves.
Only buildings, low, with colonnades; huge trees;
the Peak, now lush and verdant, bare like a moonscape.

It is cosy in the room, manageable, known;
Getting the history books in order
Before new possessors come.

People came and went about their business,
crossing the lenses of old cameras;
but they—intent on things that stayed
more permanently—
ignored them, made no record.

Will the Chinese cameras,
moving in terms of centuries, not hours,
notice us
at all?

1972

Root support

Of course, there's concrete everywhere.

But the vegetable world
still seeds and sprouts
creeps and shoots
blossoms and grows
in places.

Unaided by man,
large trees have established themselves
on high walls.

Sitting high up in double-decker buses
one admires
the gnarled network
of root support
covering large areas of wall;

the curved shapes
humanising
the straight lines of masonry

harmonised already
by the grime of passing time.

If the wall goes, the tree will die too.

Gillian Bickley For the Record

Tree, do not penetrate too vigorously
the sealing lime

Unless, facing modernity with
a withering apprehension,

you have hit on this way

of making
a bizarre suicide

look like death from natural causes.

1982

Red

There's no nonsense about that bougainvillaea.
It's just
red.
Not the same red as the stop of the traffic-light,
Nor of the high rise wall in the right middle-ground,
Nor the red of the girl's anorak or her shopping-bag.
But red. Dark red through and through.
Nothing fancy.
Not that beautiful deep purple set off with lighter purple,
Double dressed.
Just one arched arch of red flower.

1982

Chunam Plaster, Pokfulam Road

After making new roads and other improvements
designed to assist more people
live further out
and suffer the daily frustration
of travelling in
through the inefficient anguish
of landlocked cars;
men in Hong Kong
bedaub slopes that were green and grey and brown
with Chunam plaster;
designed to stop land-slips
that might make more interesting
their daily struggle
to commuters.

They experiment with colour—green and a different green
and brown—
to see which will make
this putty-coloured stretch of blandness
more harmonious

fit in more
with the grass and bushes, trees and rocks
no longer there.

Lately, they have planted bougainvillaea,
trained it to wires,
hoping it will grow and burgeon,
covering their shame
with a blaze of crimson, purple, orange.

In some parts this has happened.

Elsewhere, in the weep-holes

Gillian Bickley For the Record

intended to run-off the water
from the rain of typhoons
and gratefully accepted as homes
by the population of snakes,

seeds have directed themselves

asserting their various right

to land
possessed

when men
preferred
to live in the malarious
central district

or the thick mists
of the Peak.

1982

Old Men's Beards

Long association has made me see
the aerial roots
of big trees
like nothing so much
as the trailing uneven wisps
of an old Chinese gentleman's
beard.

1982

Waiting for Deliverance

In Kowloon Park,
on the edge, overlooking Nathan Road,
a part of the Park
planned soon to be merely
another part of the Golden Mile
of goods, baits for tourists' money;
—there—
is a concrete bunker,
a store for tools and rubbish.

Gesturing mutely toward the passers-by
sticks out a rake with six bent fingers—
a hand buried there, waiting deliverance.

1982

Chinese Gardening

Much time and thought and money
is given to practising
sophisticated horticultural arts.

Once a year, the City Hall
sponsors the display of Bonsai Trees,
the art whereby, by patient snipping,
appropriate feeding and much experience,
potential landmarks are trimmed down
to dolls'-house scale.

Also annually, Ocean Park displays
chrysanthemums
which the unwary might suppose
a new variety,
seemingly sprouting
on stiff stems
impressive heads of burnt orange, yellow and red
from one teeming root.

1982

Material Souls

Many ladies take Ikebana lessons,
calling flowers and twigs and bark
fruits and extraordinary natural finds,
"materials":

making beautiful constructs;
as they labour
to express the Universe
and come to terms with their souls.

1982

Blue Blood

Hawkers in the streets and alleys offer
carnations
dyed an ink-coloured blue.

1982

Life-saving Face

Hong Kong gardening takes place mainly in pots.
Is this a face-saving device? Failures
can be removed easily, replaced.

Or, more likely, is it akin
to the local love
of hoarding gold
and a slight hesitation
to deposit what they have earned
in the common ground of banks;

a not irrational desire

to be able to hold
what one has worked on,
to take it up and run
when the enemy—invader or developer —comes.

1982

Tobacco is an adult habit

How happily inappropriate are
the cultivated tobacco plants
in the children's playground in Robinson Road.
Their incredible sexuality:
pinkish brown outer leaves
opening
to an unfolding bright pink.

1982

Survival

Thank you trees for being there, for staying
when many of the friends you knew –
birds and butterflies – have gone;
for flourishing, even; growing old
here, where concrete buildings
are constantly knocked down.

How brave you are to survive
in a place where the air is foul
and the noise unnatural;
you, who should normally expect
to stabilise your roots
in humid humming forests,
alive with the smells
of animal and vegetable life
(not the smells of mineral death, as here).

It is good to look down a street
and, amazed, to see you there,
solid and green and cool, uncompromised
by the advertising posters on your boles;

a promise

that, since there was a past,
there may quite possibly be a future too.

1982

Comparing Notes

In England recently
I delighted in bird-song.

A blackbird sings
beautifully
outside
my parents' house.
A loud, round, sound.
Dulled by no ambient noise of human shouts
or traffic grinding on.
Free and brave and content.
Singing because this is what it does.
And if the people
in whose jasmined wall
his nest is built
take joy in it,
he may know this, or not.

Living in Hong Kong, I had forgotten
the song of birds
freely offered
in the process of living;
songs to the evening and the early sun,
songs to the spring and the glowing forsythia,
cries of alarm at cats.

Gillian Bickley For the Record

I have become accustomed to birds in cages
kept in cages because they sing so sweet

in order that they may sing and please their owner,
give him prestige and pleasure
in the midst
of other owners
of birds in cages,
whom he meets daily at special places

to compare notes.

Enormous sums are paid
to purchase them,
elaborate cages given them.
Expensive porcelain contains their water and seed.
Whole alleys of specialist shops
cater to their needs.

They are taken for walks,
their cages held
high
in their purchaser's hand,
to simulate flight.
Their cages
are perched
in the leafy trees and flowers.

And they sing too,
beautiful songs.
But somehow sophisticated.
Somehow aware
that their song
is the price of life.

Gillian Bickley For the Record

Adapted
to the cultivated taste of man.
Educated. Artistic. Unfree.

Their owners
have not spared them,
on their outings,
the plucked bodies
of tiny birds

who do not sing,

exposed for the pot.

1982

Sartor Resartus[1]

There's that woman again. That girl
with the big bum and
the voluminous trousers.

It appears she lives in the Y

and is called for
daily
by an anxious escort.

Maybe he fears

the other young people

—fashion-conscious Hong Kong,
slim and unkind—

will mob her

or tear her apart

for showing

too much side.

1982

The Exemplary Expatriate On A Monday Afternoon At Four-Thirty p.m.

He passes on home,

almost leaning backwards
in his passion
to be upright;

his silver-fringed pate
gleaming

with conscious virtue,
too liquid a lunch
and the sun
of Sunday's launch-picnic.

1982

Janus

There are times when it has a quality of glamour
—this Hong Kong—
the balmy afternoon
following a grey, cold, day.
A standing Buddhist monk
with sharp features and
inquisitive eyes—
a Westerner with shaven head.[2]

And close by the hasty walk
of a golden-curled young man
wiping the sweat from his brow.

Now now it comes to light
two ways of seeing
one world.

1982

Misfit

The raincoat I bought off a barrow
quite cheap

was clearly made
bearing in mind

a woman measuring eight inches from shoulder to middle,
six foot tall, with a sixty inch waist.

It fits me quite well.

1982

Everything Has A Price Tag

A.   How did you break your nose?
B.   I like reading too much.

A.   How d'you mean,
     you like reading too much?

B. I was walking down some steps, see,
     and the girl
     in front of me
     had the price
     on the soles
     of her shoes.

1982

One Pearl, One Plain

Knitting is popular with young girls
of a certain type.

It allows them foretastes
of their urgently desired
destiny
of physical creation

and—in their minds—
helps
bring about

a final
casting-off.

1982

A Place On The Bus

In Hong Kong
people—some people—have now learnt
about queues.
They send
their amahs
to keep a place
for them
outside the towering
blocks of flats;
where their newly-purchased
home—four hundred square feet for a family of six—
incontrovertibly asserts
their arrival in the middle class.

Having secured their place in society,
it would not do
to recreate
the ethos
of their earlier, shoving conditions,
by powerfully pushing
for a place on the transport
to ferry them to the work
that gives it them.

1982

Sign

The sign shows an arrow,
indicating,
"To the Mass Transit Railway".
It also shows a walker,
indicating
"By walking".

It points up steps.

Do they seriously consider
we would be
capable
of
some
alternative locomotion?

And if we were
would not the Mass Transit Railway be
REDUNDANT?

1982

Discrimination

Do men's lavatories smell worse
because they don't . . . can't
put the lid on it?

1982

Newsworthy

Now the obscuring screen is partially removed,
drivers who lift their eyes from their newspapers
(bought to ease the languor and anger of traffic jams)
may see a friendly sight:
a new wall in an old wall's arm.

Part of the old retaining wall
on Village Road
is being itself retained;
its heavy stones mated
to palely-grooved concrete.

Astonishing.
The Public Works Department
thus shows itself
more familiar
with Coleridge
than Holy Writ;

his accurate sighting
of the new moon
in the old moon's arm[3]
inspiring in them more confidence,
than warnings
about new wine in old bottles,
new patches on old material.[4]

Commuters, wait and see!
The daily news
may be written
in the dust
you make.
1982

Help

It sometimes seems
that Chinese restaurants
keep
quite specially
bent pairs of chopsticks—
an aid to foreigners
in living up to
their required role
of eating clumsily.

1982

Good Luck A Local Product

Who would have thought that in Hong Kong
one went in danger
of bird-waste;
that birds actually fly overhead
and drop down good luck.

The event must be a rare one:
for the Cantonese—
so versed in good luck symbols,
happy auguries—
do not acknowledge
its auspiciousness.

Now, let's analyse this scientifically.
Maybe the diet differs;
hence the waste produced.

The luck may depend on some component
present only in the British variety.

In this case, we have
not cultural difference
but accurate perception
of a product
that differs.

1982

Rain

Even the green tarpaulin
of the disguised squatter-hut
looks the brighter and cleaner for the rain.

Ah, the cumulus clouds!
rolling low on the hills, on the sea.

The trees bounce with visible life,
bursting an extra dimension
insoaked with the luxury of
yearned-for, half-forgotten, rain.

Green Chinese tiles glow,
some concrete looks scrubbed.
The air is temporarily purified;
for a time, gives more life
than it threatens.

By some chance,
green is what I am wearing
too.

1982

The Creator Commands His Own Creation

*On the first performance by the Cleveland Orchestra at the
Tenth Hong Kong Arts Festival.*

Lorin Maazel, what does it feel like
as you walk onto the stage of Hong Kong
jet-lagged

all those notes in your head
all those sounds and shapes
rhythms and moods . . .

Are you aware of the audience,
much aware of the souls
in the orchestra?

Or are you simply
immanent
with the music

heavy with the music
that you need no score
to conduct?

Aware of the crowded platform
around you
only as the plastic chaos
out of which
you will command
creation?

You <u>are</u> imperative.
Impatient to deliver
you command immediate labour.

Gillian Bickley For the Record

Joyously, with the discipline
of plenitude,
the orchestra
midwives
at your direction.

Many men
must envy you
your potency, your skill.

Upright and lithe,
single-minded, determined,
energetic and absorbed,
instructions issue from the whole of you.

Though the unsmiling face
is even grim,
your body lilts and insists,
creates by its movements
the mellow beauty
and the urgent pattern
of other men's work,
making it yours.

And then we understand.

It is not you who creates the music
but the music that creates you.

Gillian Bickley For the Record

All this magnificent sound,
intelligent and moving,
exists
to create at its centre
you.

Though you command it,
it creates you.

All present wonder at this birth.
For now you smile, relax.
You enter into approving relationships with
the first violin and cello.

The music has recreated you.

In Hong Kong too, your life is given to you.

1982

Second Thoughts

A week ago, I gave up possessions—
not the ones I have (except the useless ones)—
but the ones I don't have yet.

I cannot spare my life to care for them.
In any case I need the money.
But now I find the loophole I have left myself
is enormous.
I haven't defined the term at all.

What about tools and investments?
I must still need those?

And how many things can be defined this way?
Cars and typewriters, answer-phones and home-computers
are surely tools;

while oriental carpets, prints of Hiroshige and Thomas
Allom,
must be both:
tools to impress potential clients, and
investments against an inflationary future.

And then, self-care.
It's all very well not buying things that need *me* to care for
them.
But what about things that care for *me*?
Curling-tongs and hair-dryers, skin-cream and perfume,
an orthopoedic mattress and a suitable chair:
objects that care for my state of mind —
the very possessions I have given up.

Gillian Bickley For the Record

I am disappointed to find
my honest intentions
undermined
by experience of filling in tax returns
and the habit of cajoling bureaucrats.

I do not know how to proceed.

1982

Temptation

It seems that the temptations in the wilderness
represent a strong psychological truth.
A week ago I "gave up possessions"
and never have material objects been
so attractive.

Perhaps it was a silly decision
for someone with two fur coats, ten handbags
and thirty pairs of shoes; eight deteriorating strings
of shells and seeds that are never worn, five
pairs of shorts
and fifteen T-shirts bought cheap off barrows ditto.
Or maybe just the wrong place to implement this decision.

Hong Kong, after all, is a shopping paradise,
a place whose whole ethos cries, "buy", "buy":
Hennessy Road calls me to buy cheap bed-linen and beaded
purses.
The Italian shoe-shop is having a half-price sale.
Leather shoulder bags—just what I was looking for when I
was looking,
but couldn't find *then*—
big, sufficiently attractive, leather-lined and hence
long-lasting,
obtrude to my notice.

And even my horoscope warns me
that by being too saving of money
I am depriving myself and those around me
of pleasures I can well afford.

Gillian Bickley For the Record

Maybe I should have waited
until I had given up my job and had no salary,
rather than now when merely preparing
for so drastic a change.

It would be easier to give things up
when I can no longer afford them.

1982

The Reason For It

I am writing too much.
It is wearing me out.
I am hungry all the time.

Maybe this is why poets starve.

Poetry is not a paying profession.

If it typically creates
an unusual urge to eat
no wonder poets fail
to provide themselves
adequate nourishment.

1982

Bringing In The Tea

A sharp noise. I look. A bird on the window sill.
Has it always been there, immobile
porcelain or plaster?

Have I seen you before, long beak,
black markings on your face
and yellow breast?

And now you turn.
You look straight at me
asking yourself, Is it real
and what is it doing here so high above the ground,
looking at the yellow round cactus on the window sill
(the secretary's successful child)?

A buzzer which disturbs me does not disturb you.
But, my concentration broken, I move my head
and
you fly away.

You had not sung
but I am left for music
the grinding of the high-rise office trolley
bringing in the tea.

1970-1997

Exit

Yesterday I saw a butterfly, slightly disturbed,
but purposeful, the possibility of hysteria
only
a possibility

contradicting my inward descent into the subway

flying on a route that would take it out
as I hurried down steps that led me in.

Today, I saw a caterpillar, small and thin
possibly the same species.
Perhaps there will be a generation of butterflies
teaching us the way out.

1978-1979

Moon-Shine

In this city of multi-storeys,
I rarely look up to the sky.
"It doesn't have enough sky,"
I say to people
who ask me
What Hong Kong
Is Like;

by which I mean,
there is too much here that impedes
our vision of the light.

There aren't even many stars.

For even away from the high-rises,
out at the Village,
where bedroom windows may outlook
at the water, at quiet islands,
even here, the unseen effluvia
of all our human lives and living
obscure the distant light of stars.

This is why the city lights have such compulsion for us.
Theirs is the only nightly twinkling
we can be sure to see.
Sometimes even these are lessened
when oil is short,
and conservation wins a little point.

Gillian Bickley For the Record

Man obviously has such a need for twinkling—
to embrace the pure truth
that even after death
calm influence and disembodied
beauty
can
make warm the hearts of living men
comfort and uplift them to love of an
untouchable ideal.

But here in Hong Kong, there is nothing to look *up* to.
And so we climb the Peak and look *down*
at the city lights.

Our pleasure is in neon lights
that soon burn out,
proclaiming the busy-ness of materiality,
the purchasable pleasures of a *daily* life
things to buy and use and throw away
flesh, food and raiments.

Once a year, the Chinese climb high places
for a different purpose:
to admire the Moon.

With them they carry lanterns
representing the Moon
by candles and bright paper that can tear and burn.

This morning I looked up.

Gillian Bickley For the Record

I saw—between a corridor of buildings—
the full moon
white and alien
cloud-coloured white
with the dark shapes of mountains, deserts, plains.

"Look at the Moon!" I say, surprised, pleased.
The other early riser cannot comprehend this
this unexpected message.
She clearly thinks, "This is some strange English idiom
not learnt by those who left school after Secondary Five."

She hurries on, down into the subway, where
no light of stars will ever reach.

The moon looks out of place, an exotic visitor
downcast by lack of welcome,
bled pale by lack of understanding.

O Moon, persist, draw deep on your resources.
Compel us to regard you. Here.

1980-1982

Gillian Bickley For the Record

*On 5 April 1991, Ching Ming Festival, a family of five was
badly burned after being surrounded by a hill fire while
visiting their ancestors' graves near Liu To Village, on the
northwest of Tsing Yi Island, where the traditional
occupation is boat-building. The Husband and Wife and
their three daughters, Shui-kei, aged eleven, Shui-ki, aged
ten and Shui-ka, aged three, were all injured. The fire was
started by other grave-sweepers around mid-day, and
spread quickly to cover an area of fifty hectares. It took
ambulance-men forty-five minutes to reach the family, who
were trapped half-way up the hill. They were carried by
stretcher to the top of the hill, from where a helicopter took
them to the British Military Hospital. Their Ancestor
speaks.*

Ching Ming Festival, April the Fifth, 1991[5]

Here they come again, my family—
my grandson, my grandson's wife, my three
great grand-daughters. It is good to see them.

Although the view is good from here—I can
see the sea, where boats like those I built
pass in and out of sight; I can see the sky
expressing many moods; the sun moving
in ascending then descending arcs as years go by;
rising and setting as the days progress,
reddening then greying; warming benignly,
or—with equal heart—brutishly burning
the dry grass, combustible as tinder.

I can see the fullness of the bright round moon
at the mid-autumn festival,
the moon lady and the moon rabbit.

But I see no lanterns as I used to see;

the little children proud and happy,
timid or—though rarely—tearful. It is
a long time since my son showed me his lantern
at the festival. These children, never.
Much time has passed.

The view is good: and the comfortable
hill behind holds me embraced, secure. Yet
it is lonely here. It is good to see them.
Shiu-chi running ahead.
Shiu-kei, the eldest—more responsible—
helping her mother carry the oranges.
And Shiu-ka, I see, is talking now.
Ming-yeung, my Grandson, who bears the sucking pig,
begins to show his years. In not too long
a time, perhaps, he joins my Son, his Father,
lying apart from here; who also sees
the sea, the stars, the sky;
protected by the warm enclosing earth.

But now they talk to me; they share with me
some parts of worldly life; they eat with me
again. The smell of incense and the family
warmth return my thoughts to men.

Beyond us, lower down the hill, neighbours' families
visit their ancestors, in greater numbers
than in previous years, lighting the fragrant joss-sticks.

***

I do not want to feel this heat;
I do not want to listen to it roar,
I do not want to see this light, this burning brightness
that encircles us, too quickly coming near.
I do not care to see the childrens' fear,

Gillian Bickley For the Record

my Grandson's helplessness; the panic in their eyes.
I do not like to see their pain, to hear their screams,
to smell their burning flesh.

Running up the hill, passing through the fire,
strangers in heavy clothing come, disciplined, daring the
flames.
They raise my family skilfully, with careful speed,
dressing their burns with routine, but shocked, care.
Climbing more heavily to the as yet unlit peak,
they bear them all away.

The last I see of them,
Ming-yeung, my Grandson,
Wai-yin, his wife, Shui-chi, Shui-kei, Shui-ka,
my three great-grand-daughters,
they are lifted into the sky.

Near me, the burning grass catches, crackles
and flares. Advancing swiftly, it consumes
the suckling pig, bursting the oranges,
blackening the stone that records my name.

Rushing onwards, the fiery wall is challenged
by brave men, resists, advances, falls back,

and ultimately dies.

                        ***

I and my neighbours,
we did not ask this human sacrifice.

Once a year only, we see our family
and we know their life; turning our thoughts back
to their human world;
Then, repossessing a usual calmness of mind,

Gillian Bickley For the Record

renewing awareness of hills and sea,
conscious of our place in their existence,
we resume our sentient peace.

The view is good: and the comfortable
hill behind holds me embraced, secure.

Next year, come Ching Ming Festival again,
will there be a family to visit me,
to sustain my memories of earlier,
human, life?

From now on, and for ever,
will it be lonelier here?

1991

Gillian Bickley For the Record

Swallows[6]

I drive to work early, avoiding worse
traffic at the approach road to the Tunnel
by Lion Rock.

Yesterday, for the third time, I saw, in front
of me, a flock of birds wheeling two . . . three . . .times
in the clear early air;
practising their departure.

Their wings caught the morning sunlight as they turned
and rose, speeding together towards dense tower-blocks;
avoiding collision and death
by beating upwards suddenly,
turning,
and swinging
unanimously
back
to where originally, they grouped.

Three times they do this, before I crawl
under them, and lose sight of them.

But something puzzles me.
One part of them only
seems to separate and fly lower than the other,
between, not above, the buildings,
dangerously;
each time survives,
rejoins the group,
miraculously.

Gillian Bickley For the Record

Then I see, no miracle at all.
It is their shadows only
which swirl in and out
between the tall concrete
and deceptive glass.
Their true selves remain above,
free in the familiar sky.

And I ask, is there a parable here?
Is it the shadows only of our Hong Kong selves that
seem
to fly away
from Kai Tak;
our real
selves
remaining behind?

9 October 1997

Gillian Bickley For the Record

Soon after the return of Hong Kong, a former British Crown Colony, to Mainland China (midnight 30 June 1997), a Festival of Chinese Opera was held in Hong Kong in October 1997.

Expect it hot

Yes. It was a good idea to stage
a Festival of Chinese opera
in Hong Kong
so soon after the Handback—not Handover—
to China.

The Audience loved it.
The first one we attended—
"Assassination of the Emperor Chin"—
was performed by Hong Kong's own Hong Kong
Opera Troupe. A working-class Chinese audience
simmered and buzzed in the green plush seats,
enjoying the grand comfortable theatre
and the grandeur of *their* art-form.

When we left—half-time up and three hours
to go, our right-hand neighbours summoned
generosity and poise
to utter, "It doesn't matter",
as we squeezed, self-deprecatingly, past their knees.

Our next excursion took us to the Ko
Shan Theatre near the Airport
to see
selections from Szechuan Opera.

Gillian Bickley For the Record

"Expect it to be hot", my husband said,
punning on the Szechuan style of cookery
and his inaccurate expectation
that there would be no air-conditioning
in that distant place

and not really expecting sex and seduction at all.

October 1997

At the same Festival of Chinese Opera, held in Hong Kong in October 1997, after the return of this former British Crown Colony to Mainland China, the Chengdu Sichuan [Szechuan] Opera Theatre performed Tan Su's adaptation of the Szechuan opera, Liu Siniang, *once banned on the Mainland "for its feudal theme".   Asked about Shakespeare's* Hamlet, *Mr Tan is reported to have said; "To be or not to be is also the critical question in our play. The leading character, Madam Liu Qingti, has to decide whether to kill a dog to prepare medicine for her son."   In the original version of the opera, Madam Liu was condemned because killing a dog was an unforgivable crime in her village. She was sent to hell. "The theme was considered 'too feudal' and was banned after the new China," Mr Tan was reported to have said. "But it is such a good opera that it would be a shame if it cannot be staged. To change it or not to change it is a difficult question. But I tried to rewrite it from a modern point of view—depicting a mother's love and her challenge to social dogmas."[7]*

Whatever changes were made, we still found the message of this opera deeply disturbing. And this made us question our own cultural assumptions.

Differences

The "New China" banned it? They did rightly so
if opera confirms taste, reinforces the status quo.

Surely serving the family pet as medicine to save one's son
is laudable,
not disgusting;
the struggle of conscience with affection, pitiable,
not irreligious;
the triumph of motherly love over convention, heroic,

not anti-social.

These are the qualities **Liu Siniang** *should* assert.

Physical violence is indicated—strangling with chains,
impaling with pitchforks, slashing with choppers,
boiling in a cauldron in hell;

but symbolically—genteelly—done.

So we focus on the
moral violence
which drives it

and find it
disgusting.

But the Chinese are loving it.

Do they simply approve what they see
as a thesis on vegetarianism,

excellently played
by actors, whose skill and athleticism
make us remember the millions
that China can choose from,

to put through these paces on a wide stage,
lavishly set and costumed
with excellent
synchronisation of singer and actor,
action and musical accompaniment?

Gillian Bickley For the Record

Could we—westerners—view *Antigone*
like this,

as a thesis on disobedience;
not the conflict of two systems of values,

one superior
because personal,

the other inferior
because social?

And how would *this* Chinese audience read it?

If they watched Shaw's *Saint Joan*, or Whiting's *The
Devils*,
would they

see through
that violence
so much more naturalistically played?

and similarly
find the cultural assumptions behind *it*
obscene?

October 1997

Gillian Bickley For the Record

We left Hong Kong for a Conference in Singapore in November 1997, at a time when there was continuingly bad news about air pollution, resulting from the slash and burn farming techniques of Indonesian peasant farmers, and exacerbated by El Nino. Since one of us suffers from asthma, we were very worried about the possible air pollution we would find in Singapore.—This, by the way, was a comment which, according to one issue of The Straits Times, *published in November 1997, we would not have been able to make over the causeway, in Malaysia. We wrote to the British Council Conference organiser, for advice. We purchased the best available masks, and came ready—if not willing—to wear them. This is the poem I wrote on the plane.*

Vision

Looking out and down
through the window
through the clear water
to the shell-encrusted rocks
of the South China Sea,

I wonder,
Are those distinct shapes
and masses
really formations beneath the water?

or dry land
obscured by Indonesian smog?

I hope the pilot knows.

November 1997

Shatin Cross-roads

As I waited at the traffic lights,
which are always red,
I looked at the people crossing in front of me:

A grandfather mildly walking
with a little girl, he carrying her
pink school-bag, adorned with a bright
"Hello Kitty";

not knowing that I found
his usual behaviour unusual, admirable;

a lesson
to the American TV producer of fashion for mums;

who screamed with revulsion
at bright childish
bags that children love,
but spoil
an office worker's
image.

Sombre, smart black was what she recommends.

As they cross, pedestrians' eyes swivel to the purple
Mercedes sports car next to my beige saloon.

March 2000

Approaching Tai Po Highway, Speeding Home

Certain things are so unusual, they suggest
significance,
which they may not have.

This was the case of the fallen worker's glove,
which swelled and rose before me,
inspirited by passing cars.

A hand rising from the road three times,
in front of me, before I mowed it down.

Not, "clothed in samite, mystic, wonderful", not
brandishing a sword.[8]

—A humble, padded worker's glove, grimy and old.

But seemingly addressing me.

Did it mean, "Stop", "No entry", "Go no further", "Turn
away",
"Beware"? — "Do not choose this road!"

I must wait and see!

March 2000

Graduation

Will you write something about all of us?
the tall student shyly asks, self-deprecatingly.

— What is there to say?

That you sat in front of me for fourteen weeks,
did the assignments I requested,
spoke up when I asked you to
and bravely took the floor, when it was your turn.

You did what was required.

Some of you asked me what to think,
and a very few,
agreeing,
when I said,
"Think for yourselves",
dared to
disagree with me.

Some of you thought me unreasonable,
to expect you to read the few books set,
feeling my more proper behaviour was,
to give you handouts, model essays,
which would indirectly tip you off
what the examination questions would be,
and do them for you.

Gillian Bickley For the Record

Some of you found some enlightenment
in the foreign books I put before you, new ideas
that resonated with your personal growth.
Some of you were startled and surprised to find in foreign
lives so many social issues like your own.

You are very different
from the Hong Kong students of the
seventies, burnt and burning from the Cultural Revolution;
from the students of the eighties,
wondering what
Hong Kong under Chinese rule would be
and weeping for lost friends at Tienamen.

You have arrived at another place,
political and personal maturity
in a modern society

and are planning
responsibly to make it yours.

I wish you luck!

March 2000

Early morning at the (University of Hong Kong) campus is a special world.

Early morning at the campus is a special world.
As I start to enter it,
a briskly walking group of women,
down from the Peak,
are barely restrained
by their abrupt leader,
from challenging my slow car.

Inside the barrier, scattered individuals
and couples
possess the spacious green world,
that still remains,
interspersing the modern buildings,
that the Cusdin plan—finally effected—has presented
to thousands of new students.

Visitors returning can still trace
old paths, see replaced buildings, know where
the Lily Pond is hidden and the rare trees grow.

The morning owners of this place—built
with the Boxer Indemnity—
still believe it is all theirs.

A neat old lady is quite au fait
with the heavy glass doors
near the computer room

And an elderly couple practice tai chi
in front of the mini-bank and bookshop.

Gillian Bickley For the Record

Students still sleep in the library,
know English picked up from American films,
and yearn for future days.

Song birds express their joy
and a koel bellows.

March 2000

Through the Lion Rock Tunnel

The first time I passed through the Lion Rock Tunnel,
we emerged the other side in a different world,
steamy, relaxed, green and exciting.

A tin hut set in wasteland by the road
was the place where people then
took early breakfast,
stoking up for an excursion
further into the unknown world
of the New Territories.

A narrow road ran dangerously near
the unfenced water, now made reclaimed land.

The Chinese University was already there,
another world too.

We drove past it, parking the car
at Tai Po Kau
and following the coloured arrows
for our Sunday walk;
avoiding the places where landslips
had contradicted
the written information.

Even then, you met people
whose transistor radios

spoilt the pleasant calm
for everyone else.

Gillian Bickley For the Record

Exercise taken, differences absorbed,
we returned
to our University flats
on the Island
and the long wait
before tomorrow.

March 2000

Memories Of School: Admiration

When my teacher retired, she gave a speech
at the Old Girls' tea;
quite a long speech,
which she had carefully prepared.

One of the things she said was,
how much pleasure we girls had given her.

Not only the clever girls, she said,
though there were those:
idealists, rebels, revolutionaries,
poets and rational minds;

But beautiful girls with long fingers
and curved necks, gazing out of the window
with vacant minds;
whom she hesitated to rebuke,
breaking the charming pose.

I thought it wonderful
and wrote her an admiring letter,

to which she tactfully
replied, saying that, sometimes,
we thought more highly of people
than they deserved.

March 2000

Marital Bliss: Filed Away

I do not want one of these modern marriages
you said;

me here, you there, whizzing from place to place
with different interests and social groups.

I want us to be together.

And that is fine. I do not want that either.
I have lived too much alone, or with the remnants
others have given me.

—So that now,
fourteen years on,
sitting in a restaurant
alone, waiting for class,
is painful to me,
the minor muzak
mournfully disturbing;

and arriving home is like closing a wound.

But
there is a downside.

I have no letters from you.

Gillian Bickley For the Record

The notes and messages
you leave me
on telephone pads
are more than
routine
requires however,

and I
keep them all,
in a file that
bears your name.

I hope it never
happens that,

one day,

it is not
you
I have
to look for,

but only
a file.

March 2000

Consistency

"We don't believe in bribing children",
my Mother
announced
out of the blue:
"two shillings for each exam mark
over eighty per cent or so
as some parents do".

And yet, years later,
similarly responding
doubtless
to a conversation
with others,
you promised
—following no request, no pressure from me—
that if I passed
my three "A" level exams,

I would receive
unasked permission
to spend my own small savings
on driving lessons
during the summer.

When I failed one paper and with it the subject,
you were consistent in that too

—"No lessons for you!"

Gillian Bickley For the Record

I have wondered, every now and then,
whether,
seeing things from my perspective,
you perceived the petty impression
of misplaced power
these separated actions made.

Did you wonder
what the consequences would be,
or had been,

of fourteen years' high passes
taken for granted,

and one failure
—slightly commiserated—

made the occasion
for withdrawal
of an unasked privilege,
you had invented?

March 2000

My Father's memories

My Father's memories
are mine too
of course

—some at second hand.

His Father—a sailor—
coming home

with a hand
of bananas, then rare fruit.

The picture of camels in the desert
with palm trees
before Pyramids.

The soap-stone figures
of three monkeys
with their unregarded message,

alien then,

"Hear no Evil, See no Evil, Speak no Evil".

My Grandfather's sayings,
which I didn't much mind.

"If they cut off your hands,
you'd be dumb."

"There's none so blind
as those that won't see."

But which my mother,

Gillian Bickley For the Record

attentive hostess,
minded a lot.

"Ah, a cup of tea
. . . the best part of the meal!"

—"He wouldn't let
me
go
on a school
day-trip to France."—

My Father still resented it.

—"He wouldn't permit me
to go
to University,
though scholarships were found.
'College was good enough for your sisters.
And it's good enough for you.'"—

"Why didn't you just go?"
—"Things were different then.
"You always did what your father said."—

Years later, when I packed my trunk for Africa,
my Father refused to help.

"I'm sorry it's ended
like this,"
he said
and walked away.

Gillian Bickley For the Record

The same seeing of big things in small.
The same fear of losing your child
by physical distance.

The same result:
—but a more significant . . . —

alienation.

March 2000

School teachers

My mother dislikes
school teachers,

or so she says.
A school teacher herself,
she married one.

Her uncle, head of the village school,
rapped her knuckles
with a ruler
before the entire school.

Her aunt, his co-teacher,
was also very strict.

Her other aunt,
thoroughly respected and admired,
she nevertheless considered
bossy.

When we went away to stay
at some small hotel
somewhere,
she always gave me
strict instructions.

"If anyone asks
what your father does,
say you don't know.

"People don't like school- teachers."

Gillian Bickley For the Record

Yet what did they want me to be?—
a school- teacher.

And they take my refusal
to consider
such a career,
as a criticism
of them
and their lives.

Perhaps
I
don't like school teachers?

(Or is it
only them?)

March 2000

After a long period of heavy media advertising, Le Cadre Noir De Saumur, described as "French Equestrian Opera", was performed in Hong Kong from 12-14 May 2000. A team of seventeen horses and men gave a programme of dressage and other demonstrations of the results of the extended training of horses and men. Riding whips were much in evidence. Horses and men were accompanied by the Hong Kong Philharmonic Orchestra, conducted by a luxuriant French female guest conductor. On occasion, a female opera singer, handsomely dressed, sang an aria. In the interval, the well-trodden sand (which had been flown in to Hong Kong specially for this event), was smoothed out by a young man operating a small cart, fitted with brushes or blades, in which he sat as in an airport buggy.

We in the audience (who had paid high prices) were well behaved. We tolerated politely a first-night opening ceremony, aimed at thanking various sponsors and giving them credit for good works. These are common at high-profile charity events in Hong Kong, but it seemed unusual to expect the paying public to find this entertaining. Nevertheless, in spite of the high ticket prices, it is likely that the event was still heavily subsidised, and in this case, it was appropriate to give the audience the opportunity both to know this and to express appreciation of those who had made their entertainment feasible. On the other hand, the many guests in the VIP seats presumably had paid nothing, and this gave them a chance to show their appreciation for their free evening.

We were provided with the two Directors of Ceremonies, which are Hong Kong routine. Their script presumably aimed at giving the audience some background on what they were to see. This time, they helpfully spoke in two languages, English and Cantonese (surprisingly, not also in French).   Unfortunately, they did not concentrate on their purpose.   They sometimes both spoke at the same time, and they did not enunciate clearly enough to take into account the huge size of the Hong Kong Coliseum.   The programme did not supply this deficiency and in any case the print was difficult to read by the lighting inside.

The event could not really stand alone as a performance. It needed a narrative to give it significance, and to satisfy the audience's curiosity about the training of these horses and men, and about the background of the different individuals (both human and equine), working so hard and with such concentration before our eyes.

In the programme, the Consul General of France speaks of this event as marking, "a new and invaluable step in its bid to appeal to a larger and more popular audience".   The first night was by no means a sell-out, but, given the number of seats, it was certainly well attended, being apparently about three fifths full.   The Coliseum venue certainly implies a "popular" audience.   There are plenty of food outlets outside the building, and snacks seemed to be sold inside it.   Small children spoke without parental restraint during the performance, and early on, one unknown (French) neighbour turned round to request greater consideration.

It was an interesting experience.

Le Cadre Noir De Saumur

If I were a horse,
would I find it fine
to pace in a ring
and posture in a line?

If I were a man,
would I like a life
disciplining a horse,
removed from other strife?

If I were a child,
would I want to hush
when I want to comment,
enjoying it so much?

Musical lady on the stand,
swaying and posturing there with the band,
telling the sweepers of strings how to sound,
urging the blowers of brass to resound,

you are controlled, as you control,
your abundant dark hair bound with a bow.
Your prancing arms a *small* space embrace,
your balancing legs given minuscule space.

And we in the seats, serried in ranks,
taking relief from offices, homes, banks,
obedient we clap, fall silent, consume,
respond as directed, dance to life's tune.

May 2000

Gillian Bickley For the Record

Protection

Yes, it was a long time ago, as you said,
lying in hospital in your last days,
that I — auxiliary nurse
in buttercup uniform
with kirby-grip buttons —
massaged the bottoms of old men —
like you, now — to prevent bed-sores.

"It's called, 'doing the backs'", I tell you,
with false cheerfulness,

trying to distract you
from the embarrassments
of your illness,

the broken verbal taboos
of your illness —
the words, "urine", "bottle" and "bed-pan" —

the revelations of the nursing notes
— "confused", anxious", "incontinent" —

but above all,

from the loud silence
of the truth
you wanted to protect me from.

October 2001

Death-bed Wisdom I

"Be Ill In The Summer"

One of the things I've learnt
in my very long life
is,

If you've got to be ill,
be ill in the summer,
when the days are long
and the endless nights
are short.

October 2001

Death-bed Wisdom II

"Don't Make Assumptions"

"Don't make assumptions,
"I've learnt that too",
you said,
on your death bed.

But you gave us no hint
of the assumptions you had made
and which you now
knew to be false.

October 2001

There was a wind in the night

There was a wind in the night
and in the morning
the apple-tree
— long rotten within —
and waiting the gardener's decision
that the time was right
to cut it down,
had fallen.

Delaying (as I thought)
the Senior Gardener's decision,

meshing you still to this life,
I told you of this, and
asked, "What shall we put
in its place?—

"Another apple tree? . . .
"A fruit tree of a different sort?"

I was glad to see that you
focussed on the matter,

returned
from your careful preoccupation,

forgot to forget the pain,
stopped ignoring the discomfort
of a wet bed
oxygen tube
bed sores
haemorrage
oedemous and weeping arm
cancer

Gillian Bickley For the Record

coming death.

"Could do", you said, so quietly;

then let go your care
for your so well tended garden —

its lawns, bright pansies, dahlias,
lavender and rosemary —

and called for nurses,
begging the small comfort they might
bring you,

rythmically repeating
"please, please, please, please, please, please, please,
please".

At ease, Daddy.

We will plant your tree again
for you.

That is all we can do
now.

October 2001

The Other Families

The other families were so humbly passive,
asking for nothing,
doing nothing,

they made me feel like a champion
when I drew the blinds slightly
to shield my father

from the glare
of the autumn afternoon sun,

asking them first, of course,
if anyone minded

if I did.

The other side of the ward
was just as bad.

"Why don't you draw yours too?"
I asked the second wife of the
sometimes truculent man
opposite.

"<u>You</u> do it," she said,
"Then <u>you</u> can get into trouble".
So I did.

Gillian Bickley For the Record

In a way, I was glad
when <u>his</u> daughter, <u>her</u> step-daughter,
arrived, looked and exclaimed,
"'Ere! Where's me Dad's roses?"

and when a nurse came along
on some routine duty
repeated the same to her.

"Where's me Dad's roses?
A dozen red roses.
I only bought
them yesterday."

And the young nurse remembered,
"Oh yes, they've gone
"to be
"watered".

And soon brought them
back:
<u>his</u> daughter's proclamation
to the world
of <u>her</u> concern and love.

October 2001

An intense desire to be oneself

A few years ago,
a millipede tickled
over
my bare shoulder
in bed
and then marched onto you,

who resisted and touched it
and it
bit you

— "quite painful", you said —
and we spent the rest of the night
in anxious alarm

and the next night,
not finding the creature.

So quite naturally,
when it turned up
in my bath,
I was pleased

and determined
to remove the cause
of our ridiculous and so far
helpless
fear.

But that multi-footed, inch-long,
personality
was equally
determined.
It would not

be hosed down the plug-hole
or drowned
or battered
to death.

And even when,
disgusted with myself,
I cut it in half (not easy to do)
with my nail-scissors,
it still manifested
an intense desire to be itself.

***

The six men in this ward do the same.
They refuse to surrender their wills, their differences.
They refuse to dissolve their sugar or salt
in the cleansing water of this hospital's routine.

They resist
— for a longish
and heroic
while —
a giant's attempt

to destroy <u>them</u>
by all means.

Showing they do not
want
to become
a drop
in the infinite ocean
or to rejoin their source, the sea.
The Christian
assertion

that
the personality
survives
after death

is proved
by this
to be pure observation
with no absolute need
for a certain faith
at all.

October 2001

Holding Hands: I

The wards had a common corridor,
open to them all.

And visitors to inner wards
passed the sufferers
in the outer.

Too hard to march past,
single-mindedly
intent
on the person
who was one's reason
to be there.

At least greet
by quick smiles of good will
those you pass.

A frail old lady
with sweet face
responds to my passing smile.

"Would you help me to put this on?"
she mildly asks, and I do.
"Is it a nebuliser?" She nods.
"Do we switch this on?" I indicate a box.
She is helplessly unsure.

"I'll call a nurse to let you know", I say
and hurry on, lest I neglect my own one person,
at least equally needy,
among these frightened many.

Gillian Bickley For the Record

Next day, a worried younger lady,
with the same sweet face,
is visiting her.

Next day again, a new young patient
occupies the opposite bed.
The least sick and the sickest among the six.

And we smile too.
Next day, the two sit close together,
the young woman holding the old lady's hand,
stroking it gently with great kindness.

Next day, the old lady is gone.
"What happened to that old lady?" I ask the young woman.
"She died."
The tears come to both our eyes.
"You were really nice to her," I say.
"She was a nice lady", the young patient said.
"It's a pity she died."

October 2001

Holding hands: II

Your much younger friend held your hand
for quite a while
and I was surprised
that you accepted
the sympathy he conveyed
without words
in this way.

You, always so scornful
(surely I remember right)
of anything sissy,
anything not entirely masculine.

Of course, we held your hand too,
from time to time,
but not too much,
lest we suggest fear of finality,
by conveying too much significance;

encouraging fond
misinterpretation
and false hope
that we offered
merely sympathy
for great suffering.

So I think
we should all
hold the hands
of friends and strangers
in their fear and pain

Gillian Bickley For the Record

hoping
that other
friends and strangers
in their turn
will act for us,

will hold the hands
and comfort
those
we love the most.

October 2001

Stripes

Wearing a pink and white
striped shirt
and matching pink tie,
his eye fixed
on the
orange with lemon-yellow
striped waistcoat
of the USD worker,

as he washed, dried, and polished
the USD garbage container
in the Star Ferry
pedestrian underpass;

doubtless congratulating himself
that he could
make
his own sartorial decisions.

18 April 2002

Flower de lune

Slender as a
single chrysanthemum
petal,

the new moon
lies on her back,

anticipating
the roundness
that will come.

17 April 2002

A Talk Given to the English Society of the University of Hong Kong, 19 April 2002.[9]

Literary Odyssey in Hong Kong: a Personal Narrative

When I was invited to speak to you as part of the English Festival 2002, with the theme "English for All, All for English?", it was suggested that I might share with you my observations on the literary scene in Hong Kong.

I received this invitation on 6 April *this year.* At first, I felt overwhelmed by the size of the task that had been suggested to me, impossible to address rigorously in even thirteen *full* days work, let alone thirteen days, already, to be truthful, occupied quite fully! But congratulations on suggesting a really interesting Ph.D. topic! And I'm quite serious about this. It really would be a most interesting Ph.D. topic. But one, perhaps, needing bilingual, or even trilingual, skills; because much of the literary activity in Hong Kong does take place in Chinese. And this leads us to the title of your English Festival 2002, "English For All, All for English?" With the first part, I have no argument, English certainly is available to all who wish to use it; but whether all do wish to use English is another matter. I'm reminded of the fact that two famous English poets of the seventeenth century, John Milton and Andrew Marvell, had, among their occupations, successively, "Latin Secretary" to the Council of State, formed after the execution of King Charles the first of England. And each in fact has left a body of literary works in Latin. As you may know, formal education, at that time, in England, and indeed in Europe as a whole, was heavily focussed on learning the Latin language and studying works written in the Latin language. The choice for educated writers, then, in England, was, whether to write in English or in Latin. The work of those who chose Latin would not now be accessible to many people. It is true that the work of those who wrote in English is not entirely accessible either, because the range of knowledge that they draw on, and expect their readers to draw on too, is different from our knowledge today, as are many of their, and our, cultural assumptions; but, certainly, their work is more accessible to the majority today than anything written in Latin!

Those writing in Hong Kong today may not express the choice between English and Chinese in the same way, but there is no doubt that, for the majority, who are Chinese writers, many of whom may be bilingual in Chinese and English, there is such a choice. I cannot predict which would be the right choice, for writers who are looking to the future for a readership. Considering the present, the choice will be based on the audience one wishes to address: is it Chinese or English, which their potential, or specifically intended, readers, know? It will also be based on the subject matter one has, and the style and language which best convey what one wishes to say.

As may be obvious, but which is not necessarily obvious in relation to every person who looks somewhat like myself (some westerners, I am told by my Chinese colleagues, have excellent Chinese language skills), I personally do not have such a choice. And this leads me on to another area of literary life in Hong Kong, that part which you undoubtedly had in mind when you wrote me your letter, inviting me to speak to you today.

A fairly recent phenomenon, demonstrated by the other Festival taking place in Hong Kong this week, the Hong Kong International Literary Festival, now in its second year, is the obvious growth of an English-language literary scene in Hong Kong. As long as I have been in Hong Kong, that is, since 1970, as far as my personal knowledge goes, there has been an interest certainly among a few. One English language literary journal, to which I contributed, was created in the 1970's, but died through lack of support, after a short time. It was not the first such attempt. A recently established literary journal seems likely to continue into the forseeable future, and there is a plan for an *Asian Review of Books*, already an online publication, to become a more formal online newspaper. There is a Writers' Circle, a Women in Publishing Society, to both of which I belong, various book clubs (I belong to one of these), a poetry group, and I am sure many other such groups in town. Recently, Alex Kuo, known as an American Chinese writer, but with roots in Hong Kong, was awarded the American Book Prize. His book was published in Hong Kong and we think this is the first time that any book published in Hong Kong has received such honour. All activities need icons for inspiration. Alex Kuo's success with this Hong Kong published book may lead others to adopt <u>him</u> as an icon to inspire other "writers in English with Hong Kong roots". You yourselves, in the English Department of the University of Hong Kong, have another potential icon living with you day by day, Shirley Lim, a successor with a difference to that earlier icon of the Department, English-born English-language poet, Edmund Blunden. The University of Hong Kong is lucky also to have Agnes Lam, Associate Professor in the English Centre, a sensitive and exceptionally moving poet.

When I accepted your invitation, and gave you my title, "Literary Odyssey in Hong Kong: a Personal Narrative", I thought that, by telling you about my own writing, during my time in Hong Kong since 1970, I could reflect—talking about what I know best—my own experience, a development which might be taken as emblematic of any non Chinese writer's experience in Hong Kong during this period. I thought I would say that Odysseus, whose story the *Odyssey* mainly is, having left home to do a job of work (to join the seige of Troy), had difficulty returning home after the work was done, being seduced by many interesting experiences on the way. And I thought I would mention to you, not my physical Odyssey, from England to Hong Kong and the delay in my return to where I came, for similar reasons — the interesting experiences and people away from home — but my *literary* Odyssey, *among literary genres.* — And of course I use this famous example in all humility, simply as a quick way to signal my meaning. — I thought I would mention that I wrote my first poem when I was seven, sent my first prose fiction to a major English publisher at the age of eleven, my first academic work to a Hong Kong publisher at something like twenty-nine, and so on; but that I then became involved with writing textbooks for Hong Kong, with research about Hong Kong, particularly the history of Hong Kong creative writing in English published in Hong Kong, the history of the western education system in Hong Kong and its personalities, and a couple of years ago, with bringing back to attention Hong Kong's only known contribution to date to the genre of future war fiction, *The Back Door*, first published in 1897, republished as *Hong Kong Invaded1 A '97 Nightmare*, by the University of Hong Kong Press. But every now and then, when I have had time, I have gone back to the first genre I turned my hand to, and composed a poem or even several poems in fifteen minutes or a couple of days. And my next work may perhaps be a small publication with various poems written in Hong Kong, some attempting to exercise what Keats called "negative capability", trying to enter into the minds of others (which *The Golden Needle*, my biography of the founder of Hong Kong Government Education, Frederick Stewart, also of course attempts to do). Some try to capture something that I saw in Hong Kong and the connection it made with something else in my mind. Some express reactions to experiences which, although they owe nothing to Hong Kong directly, are in fact the product of the fact that I live in Hong Kong.

My new book, published this week, *The Development of Education in Hong Kong, 1841-1897: as revealed by the Early Education Reports of the Hong Kong Government, 1848-1896*, makes available some of the sources that I used for my work on the nineteenth century history of Hong Kong education. Part of my intention was to make it possible for others, without the labour of finding materials that I myself experienced, to take up this important subject for themselves. And this may release me from rolling a stone like Sisyphus up the hill, day in, day out, only to have to begin to roll it up again the following day.

Sometimes in the past several years, I, or my husband, Verner Bickley, who is equally interested in the topic and much more influential, have been able to convince a couple of key people to take a historical perspective, say, about the standard of English in Hong Kong, based on our research into the records and our writing over a fifteen years period, and to revise the opinions they held, based on hearsay and anecdotal experience. But, no sooner has this been achieved, than they move to a different position, new people arrive in Hong Kong, fresh people take key positions, the old inaccurate points of view are repeated and reinstated, and our information and arguments need to be presented all over again. I very much hope that this new book, which makes an important body of archival material on Hong Kong, particularly the history of Hong Kong education, available to the general public as well as to scholars, policy-makers and educationists, will in time lift the general popular knowledge on this important topic to a higher level.

If this happens, maybe my previously occasional return to the genre of poetry, the genre from which I departed on an Odyssey of non-fiction and academic work, will be a return home at least as permanent as Odysseus made. — And I have to admit that, as poignantly shown in English poet Alfred, Lord Tennyson's poem, *Ulysses*, Odysseus may have found it impossible to stay at home, but — as Tennyson suggests in his poem — set out again, after some time, on further, or repeated, adventures.

I spoke earlier about the choice — whether to write in English or Chinese — facing English/Chinese bilingual writers in Hong Kong today (I assume these bilingual Hong Kong writers are mainly Chinese people). But what about the choice for non-Chinese writers, monolingual in English, living in Hong Kong? Although they have no choice of language, they have a choice of subject.

"Write about what you know": this is early advice given to any beginning writer. "Write the book that only you can write": this is also advice often given. And both are obviously most excellent advice, the second being the more inspirational.

But what the monolingual writer living in Hong Kong knows is increasingly Hong Kong, or their own experience within a Hong Kong context. And the book or other writing that only he or she can write is increasingly a book that owes much to Hong Kong. Writing on these subjects is thus strongly indicated (as the instructions on bottles of medicine, seeking to do us good, express themselves).

But writers do not write only to express themselves, they write to communicate with others, even to influence them, if only a little bit. But influence requires access; access requires publication (in one form or another); publication requires publishers (of one sort or another); publishers require money; money comes from the sale of literary work to readers.

I am not going to speak about the xerox machine, a wonderful invention which has made all our lives easier and more efficient, or about the fact that the purchaser of literary work is an important contributor to the literary scene, or the fact that you students now and in the future are the inheritors of the responsibility to support the literary scene, at least by the purchase of literary works, including contemporary literary works, not yet affirmed by the test of time.

But I *am* going to speak about the readership for works in English by non-Chinese writers, living in Hong Kong, writing about what they know, writing the book that only they can write. I do not think they can be sustained permanently by the Hong Kong non-Chinese readership only, which is very small. They need the interest and encouragement that their Chinese fellow residents can give them; and in this also, you students can — I would like to say "must" — lead the way. As an educated élite, living in an international city which aspires to be a world city, it is surely reasonable to suppose that you do or could take an interest in residents of international origins, living in your midst, at least as much as in those who visit for a while or always live in a different place? And I am very encouraged by your invitation to me to speak to you today, which shows that this group at least, does take an interest in writers among this minority group, like myself.

Of course, there *is* an international market. And some books with Hong Kong roots have already done well in this market. A "block-buster" like James Clavell's *Taipan*. Richard Mason's *The World of Suzie Wong*. Han Suyin's *A Many Splendored Thing* (the film, *Love is a Many Splendoured Thing*, is of course based on this). But a place in the international market for writing with Hong Kong roots is by no means assured. Christopher New's books have taken <u>decades</u> to become more current. (As you will know, Christopher New was a member of this University, of the Philosophy Department, for a large number of years.) And for every book that does become successful, even very successful in the international market, hundreds are necessary as the mulch — the nourishing base

— from which they can grow. It is these hundreds, even thousands, of good works, written in English and with Hong Kong roots, read and appreciated by Hong Kong people as a whole, which are needed before Hong Kong can have a lasting international voice in the international literary world. And, to achieve this, the writers in our midst that there are now, and the writers in the future, that there may be, need an interested readership, working in partnership with themselves to grow their works and give not only themselves but all of us a voice that is heard.

Thank you for listening to my voice today.

FROM THE REVIEWS

"Gillian Bickley has the sharp eye and strong stomach of the true realist. ... brilliantly observed.... 'Tobacco' is about as close as any poet comes to word-perfect... Not even the American minimalist William Carlos Williams could zero in on and capture a detail with more panache. ...A thought-provoking and entertaining contribution to Hong Kong literature. Bickley succeeds in conveying the character of the Fragrant Harbour with humorous rigour."
— David Wilson, *Sunday Morning Post,* 21 September 2003

"In *For the Record and other Poems of Hong Kong,* Gillian Bickley inhabits a world of movement, traffic, construction and buildings, but her poetry sees through this to a nature of flying, singing birds and lush green trees existing in harmony or sometimes at odds with modern day Hong Kong. Her work offers a counterpoint of the survival and continuity of nature against which our busy everyday lives are measured. Bickley's Hong Kong is both a universal and a personal one and, like Italo Calvino's book *The City,* she captures a Hong Kong of the mind, the one city that we all share as a physical space against the myriad cities that we experience and perceive distinctly as our own. She skillfully fuses the human and the natural world".
— Dave McKirdy, poet, *The Asian Review of Books,* 21 September 2003.

"*For the Record* is a perceptive account of life and people mostly in Hong Kong, rendered with empathy, humour and surprise. A songbird in a cage, old ladies on their morning walk through a campus, a patient holding the hand of another in a hospital ward can all inspire Gillian Bickley to poetry."— Agnes Lam.

"... her work is fresh, insightful and in rhythm with the sensitivities of a community passing through a period of political and social change. More significantly, it is an important contribution to the evolution of cross-cultural poetry in, and about, Hong Kong. ... she is perhaps at her best in describing people and commonplace events in Hong Kong. ... She paints a rich and textured canvas. Rain captures a squatter village after a downpour. Moon-Shine contrasts the glowing lights of the city with the moon peeping between a corridor of high-rise buildings. ...
Dr Bickley will rekindle memories for many who lived in Hong Kong; crowded streets and concrete; ferries and flower markets; the Peak and paddy fields; trams and temple bells - and, of course, the remarkable Chinese people who live in this special place.
—Ian Wotherspoon,OSPA, nd.

"Very familiar with the local ways of doing things, lifestyle and city environment, [Bickley] observes the place from different perspectives -- from that of a poet, a Westerner, a teacher, a daughter, a woman. . . . Bickley's work is fun to read. She is an expatriate, but sometimes with a local perspective."—Cindy Chu, Book Review, *Hong Kong Journal of Modern Chinese History*, Modern Chinese History Society of Hong Kong, 2004, No. 2.

Notes

[1] The title refers to Nineteenth Century English writer, Thomas Carlyle's, work, "Sartor Resartus" ("The tailor repatched"). In this influential work, Carlyle uses clothes as a metaphor for human morals and institutions, suggesting that they also are, or can be, changed as the whims of the age and fashion dictate.

[2] I saw this western monk again (on the Mass Transit Railway (MTR)) shortly before *For the Record* was first published in 2003. I didn't quite pluck up courage, at the time, to tell him about this poem. I saw him again many months later and did mention it to him. I do not know whether he has ever read it, however!

[3] An inaccurate recall of the source, which is, in fact, not Coleridge (whose writing does have frequent references to the moon), but the anonymous seventeenth century ballad, "Sir Patrick Spens", which contains the lines, "I saw the new moon late yestreen [yesterday evening]/ With the old moon in her arm".

[4] Saint Matthew's Gospel, Chapter 9, verses 16-17.

[5] First published in a Hong Kong Baptist University English Society publication.

[6] First published in *Dimsum*, "A Journal of Good Reading".

[7] *South China Morning Post*, [21?] October 1997, p. 3.

[8] A reference to Alfred, Lord Tennyson's poem, "The Death of Arthur".

[9] Talk organised by Mr Juan Castillo, Chairperson of the English Society, and Mr Brian Tsui and held on 15-19 April, as part of the English Festival 2002, "English For All, All for English?"

ABOUT PROVERSE HONG KONG

Proverse Hong Kong is based in Hong Kong with long-term and expanding regional and international connections.

Proverse has published novels, novellas, fictionalized autobiography, non-fiction (including autobiography, biography, history, memoirs, sport, travel narratives), single-author poetry collections, children's, teens / young adult and academic books. Other interests include diaries, and academic works in the humanities, social sciences, cultural studies, linguistics and education. Some Proverse books have accompanying audio texts. Some are translated into Chinese.

Proverse welcomes authors who have a story to tell, wisdom, perceptions or information to convey, a person they want to memorialize, a neglect they want to remedy, a record they want to correct, a strong interest that they want to share, skills they want to teach, and who consciously seek to make a contribution to society in an informative, interesting and well-written way. Proverse works with texts by non-native-speaker writers of English as well as by native English-speaking writers.

The name, "Proverse", combines the words "prose" and "verse" and is pronounced accordingly.

THE PROVERSE PRIZES

Proverse administers two annual international literary prizes, one for a book-length work of unpublished fiction, non-fiction or poetry submitted in English (may be a translation) and one for a single poem (no more than 30 lines long), submitted and previously unpublished in English (may be a translation). These two prizes were first administered in 2009 and 2016 respectively. In the case of both prizes, entries are received from around the world, as well as from Hong Kong.

Please refer to the year-specific Entry Forms with Terms & Conditions, which are uploaded no later than April each year onto the Proverse Hong Kong website: <https://www.proversepublishing.com>.

The free Proverse E-Newsletter includes ongoing information about the Proverse Prize.

To be put on the E-Newsletter mailing-list, email: info@proversepublishing.com with your request.

SOME POETRY AND POETRY COLLECTIONS
Published by Proverse Hong Kong

Alphabet, by Andrew S. Guthrie. 2015.

Astra and Sebastian, by L.W. Illsley. 2011.

Bliss of Bewilderment, by Birgit Bunzel Linder. 2017.

The Burning Lake, by Jonathan Locke Hart. 2016.

Celestial Promise, by Hayley Ann Solomon. 2017.

Chasing light, by Patricia Glinton Meicholas. 2013.

China suite and other poems,
by Gillian Bickley. 2009.

Epochal Reckonings, by J.P. Linstroth, 2020.

For the record and other poems of Hong Kong,
by Gillian Bickley. 2003.

Frida Kahlo's cry and other poems,
by Laura Solomon. 2015.

Grandfather's Robin, by Gillian Bickley, 2020.

Heart to Heart: Poems, by Patty Ho. 2010.

Home, away, elsewhere,
by Vaughan Rapatahana. 2011.

Hong Kong Growing Pains, by Jon Ng. 2020.

Immortelle and bhandaaraa poems,
by Lelawattee Manoo-Rahming. 2011.

In vitro, by Laura Solomon. 2nd ed. 2014.

Irreverent poems for pretentious people,
by Henrik Hoeg. 2016.

The layers between (essays and poems),
by Celia Claase. 2015.

Of leaves & ashes, by Patty Ho. 2016.

Life Lines, by Shahilla Shariff. 2011.

*Mingled voices: the international Proverse Poetry Prize
anthology 2016*, edited by Gillian and Verner Bickley. 2017.

*Mingled voices 2: the international Proverse Poetry Prize
anthology 2017*, edited by Gillian and Verner Bickley. 2018.

*Mingled voices 3: the international Proverse Poetry Prize
anthology 2018*, edited by Gillian and Verner Bickley. 2019.

*Mingled voices 4: the international Proverse Poetry Prize
anthology 2019*, edited by Gillian and Verner Bickley. 2020.

*Mingled voices 5: the international Proverse Poetry Prize
anthology 20120* edited by Gillian and Verner Bickley. 2021.
(Scheduled)

Moving house and other poems from Hong Kong,
by Gillian Bickley. 2005.

Over the Years: Selected Collected Poems, 1972-2015,
by Gillian Bickley. 2017.

Painting the borrowed house: poems,
by Kate Rogers. 2008.

Perceptions, by Gillian Bickley. 2012.

Poems from the Wilderness, by Jack Mayer, 2020.

Rain on the pacific coast, by Elbert Siu Ping Lee. 2013.

refrain, by Jason S. Polley. 2010.

Savage Charm, by Ahmed Elbeshlawy. 2019.

Shadow play, by James Norcliffe. 2012.

Shadows in deferment, by Birgit Bunzel Linder. 2013.

Shifting sands, by Deepa Vanjani. 2016.

Sightings: a collection of poetry, with an essay, 'communicating poems', by Gillian Bickley. 2007.

Smoked pearl: poems of Hong Kong and beyond, by Akin Jeje (Akinsola Olufemi Jeje). 2010.

Of symbols misused, by Mary-Jane Newton. 2011.

The Hummingbird Sometimes Flies Backwards, by D.J. Hamilton. 2019.

The Year of the Apparitions, by José Manuel Sevilla. 2020.

Unlocking, by Mary-Jane Newton. March 2014.

Violet, by Carolina Ilica. March 2019.

Wonder, lust & itchy feet, by Sally Dellow. 2011.

POETRY: CHINESE LANGUAGE

For the record and other poems of Hong Kong, by Gillian Bickley. Translated by Simon Chow. Various E-book editions. 2010, 2021.

Moving house and other poems from Hong Kong, translated into Chinese, with additional material, by Gillian Bickley. Edited by Tony Ming-Tak Yip. Translated by Tony Yip & others. 2008.

POETRY: ITALIAN TRANSLATIONS

Avvistamenti, pensieri e sentimenti:collezione de poesie scelte 1972-2015, da Gillian Bickley, Tradutto da: Luisa Ternau, 2020.

POETRY: ENGLISH-ITALIAN
BILINGUAL EDITION

Avvistamenti, pensieri e sentimenti: Collezione di poesie scelte 1972-2015. Edizione bilingue (inglese/italiano), da Gillian Bickley, Tradutto da: Luisa Ternau

~~~
~~~

AVAILABILITY

Proverse books are available in Hong Kong and internationally
from our Hong Kong-based distributor,
The Chinese University Press,
www.cup.cuhk.edu.hk

You will find information about most Proverse titles in a
dedicated section of the CUP website:
https://cup.cuhk.edu.hk/index.php?route=product/category&path
=59_68_171

Most titles can be ordered online from amazon
(various countries)
and other online retailers.

Ebooks

Most of our titles are available also as Ebooks.

Stock-holding retailers

Hong Kong (CUP, Bookazine)
Canada (Elizabeth Campbell Books),
Andorra (Llibreria La Puça, La Llibreria).

Orders may be made from bookshops

in the UK and elsewhere.

Enquiries

Proverse Hong Kong,
https://www.proversepublishing.com
info@proversepublishing.com

FIND OUT MORE ABOUT PROVERSE AUTHORS, BOOKS, EVENTS AND LITERARY PRIZES

Website: https://www.proversepublishing.com

Twitter handle: @Proversebooks

Facebook: facebook.com/ProversePress

E-Newsletter

For a free subscription, send your request to
info@proversepublishing.com.

Youtube channel

https://www.youtube.com/channel/UCxMvyKOp7o4MWQvsIN
0FdWQ

This channel highlights poets and authors whom Proverse Press has published and also the work of Proverse itself (including our annual Spring and Autumn award and book-launch events). Proverse is a general publisher based in Hong Kong, publishing local and international authors with local and international content, including: English-language and translated literary novels, short story and poetry collections, detective stories, mysteries and thrillers, non-fiction (biography, memoirs, travel, china missionary, education and law-court history; source materials including annotated archival transcriptions) ; poetry anthologies; young adult fiction; books for students; academic studies (mainly with a Hong Kong and Hong Kong China focus). More information: www.proversepublishing.com The channel also has some elements, personal to the publishers and editors -- Hong Kong and Andorra sounds, scenes and events, for example -- inspiration and fuel for literary work.

To receive notice of the new release of videos, subscribe to the following Youtube channel (no charge).

www.ingramcontent.com/pod-product-compliance
Lightning Source LLC
Chambersburg PA
CBHW050538160726
48003CB00002B/661